TERCENTENARY COMMISSION OF THE
STATE OF CONNECTICUT

COMMITTEE ON
HISTORICAL PUBLICATIONS

Hitchcock Chairs

TERCENTENARY COMMISSION OF THE
STATE OF CONNECTICUT

COMMITTEE ON HISTORICAL PUBLICATIONS

Hitchcock Chairs

MABEL ROBERTS MOORE

O N the west branch of the Farmington River, tucked in near the corners of four towns, Hartland, Colebrook, Winchester, and Barkhamsted, was the little settlement of Hitchcocksville, named in honor of Lambert Hitchcock, maker of the well-known chairs that bear his name.

Lambert Hitchcock was born June 28, 1795, at Cheshire, Connecticut, a son of John Lee Hitchcock, a Revolutionary soldier, who was lost at sea in December, 1801, and a descendant of Matthias Hitchcock, who came from London to Boston on the *Susan and Ellen* in the spring of 1635. In 1639 he was in New Haven, where his name appears among the original signers of the "foundamehtal agreement made on the 4th of the fowerth moneth, called June, 1639."

In 1818 Lambert Hitchcock, who was a typical Yankee, settled in this little town of Barkhamsted and established a cabinet and chair factory which became the leading industry of the town. At first he made only parts

I

of chairs which he shipped in large quantities to Charleston, South Carolina and other points in the South. His business grew from the first, and by 1821 a small settlement had grown up around his factory which was given the name of Hitchcocksville.

After a few years Lambert Hitchcock gave up the shipment of chair parts, and devoted himself exclusively to the making of chairs, and put out a product that he sold in large quantities at a reasonable price. In connection with this young industry it is interesting to know that from 1810 to about 1815 the New York City Directory carried advertisements of "Fancy Chairs," and in 1825 there was a "Master Chair Makers' Society" formed. At the opening of the Erie Canal, in 1825, more than 200 men employed in making "fancy chairs" marched in the parade, carrying banners picturing decorated chairs, with the inscriptions, "By Industry We Thrive," and "Rest for the Weary."

Lambert Hitchcock was probably the originator of the sturdy, distinctive type of chairs that bear his name. The design of the chair is simple, but the same general characteristics are shown in all the many types. The two front legs are strong and firm, and the rung between them is nicely turned, while the rest of the parts are simply made. The backs have a curved top, and a broad, gently curved back-slat, usually with a narrower cross-piece, while the uprights are a continuation of the legs. The seats are wider at the front than at the back, with a rounded edge. There are many variations of these backs. Some with "cut-out" back-slats, which are a rarer type; some with "pillow-top" piece, some with the round and some with the crest or "cut-in" oval, while others show the "turtle back." Two chairs of a type that has not been credited to Hitchcock, one a straight chair and one a rocker, have recently been found bearing the "L. Hitchcock" stencil, showing a curved back and upright rounds, a style found in kitchens all through Connecticut a hundred years ago. These chairs, which are still in their original condition, are painted black, with slight grainings, with here and there the red of the first coat of paint showing through.

The first Hitchcock chairs probably had the rush seat, but very soon were added the cane and solid wooden seats. These three styles of seats were made for many years, as is proven by the stenciling on the back, and contradicts statements sometimes made that the cane seat was a much later product. At the Hitchcock factory was made a line of the true "Boston" rockers, both the large and small size, as well as the child's tiny Boston, with the rolling seat and rolling crest; also the cradle settees, or Cape Cod rockers, as they were sometimes called—that last word in modern convenience in 1825, when the baby could be placed on a pillow at one end of the settee, while the mother could sit on the other end and attend to her knitting or other work, and gently rock the baby and herself.

Of all the many types of chairs put out by Lambert Hitchcock, probably the rarest of all is the high back arm-chair with rockers, which shows nicely turned legs and rungs, as is characteristic of all of these chairs. The very high back has the "pillow" top round, while the slat below is unusually narrow, as is the slat at the base of the back. These are connected with four beautifully shaped arrow uprights. The arms, like the legs, are strong and robust, and extend below the rush seat; the rockers are short and stubby; the original decorations are conventional, showing softly faded colors in blue, gold, and gray. Lambert Hitchcock was one of the first, and possi-

3

bly the first, to turn out rocking-chairs as a factory product.

Rocking-chairs were known, of course, much earlier than Hitchcock's time, but there is a family tradition, confirmed by the statement of older people, that up to the time Lambert Hitchcock manufactured chairs, the rockers were a separate item that were added to the straight chair. He put out several different styles of children's chairs. Besides his children's "Bostons," one stout little armchair in the Winchester Historical Society is undecorated, was originally painted brown, and was bought at the Hitchcock factory for "Little Susan," six months old, at the price of fifty cents.

The decorations were one of the features that contributed to the popularity of these chairs. The stenciled designs were many times of the conventionalized fruit and leaf pattern, although we often find a basket of fruit containing pears and plums, or a bunch of grapes with leaves and a rose, and then again a fountain with birds drinking. One of the favorite designs, and a very lovely one, was the "Horn of Plenty," of which Hitchcock used several variations.

On Lambert Hitchcock's chairs, across the back of the seat on the narrow strip, was always placed the stencil of the maker, "L. Hitchcock, Hitchcocksville, Connecticut, Warranted," usually all on one line. Mr. Hitchcock was very particular as to the wood used in his chairs, allowing no knots or any imperfect thing to pass. The "Warranted" implied that they were built on honor, as 100 years of service have proven.

The stencils used were cut from very strong but light weight paper, with a design of very small checks, overlaid by blocks an inch square, whereby the stenciling was easily kept on a straight line.

4

About 1826 Lambert Hitchcock built a large brick factory, three stories high, with a cupola, which at that time was one of the big buildings of that section. Here in the up-to-date factory was added a large force of workers, 100 or more men, women, and children being employed. The women did all of the decorating of these chairs at a time when there was little work that a woman could do outside the home, although it is known that two women in this little village at this time did "tailoring" for their neighbors. The decorations were applied by using the fingers dipped first in oil, then in dry bronze or gold powder, before the part to be decorated was entirely dry, then rubbing lightly over the stencil, and later touching in the bit of color with a brush. It is said that the tips of the fingers of these women who did the decorating became as hard as boards.

Many children were employed at the factory, putting the first coat of paint on the chairs, which was always a deep red. In many of the well-worn chairs, especially the ones with the wooden seats, this red is often detected.

Business was brisk at the Hitchcocksville factory. The newspapers of the times carried many advertisements by merchants of the popular "Hitchcock chairs, Bamboo, flag and wood seats, warranted well manufactured." All went well with Lambert Hitchcock until about 1828, when the clouds began to gather, and on the twentieth of July, 1829, he was forced into bankruptcy, as a "consequence of repeated losses and misfortunes" with liabilities of $21,525.31. Of interest is the inventory of the stock, showing the scale on which he had carried on his business. It consisted principally of the following articles: "about fifteen hundred chairs in my factory in Hitchcocksville: about fifteen hundred in the hands of B. Hudson Company, of Hartford: about five hundred in the hands of Joel Atwater and Sons in New Haven: also large quantities of chairs in different markets for sale. Also five horses, wagons, carriages, harnesses. Also a large quantity of stock for the manufacture of chairs in the hands of the Warden of The State's Prison in Wethersfield: a large quantity of stock, machinery and tools in my chair factory at Hitchcocksville, a large quantity of lumber in and about the same—a large quantity of stock now in Hartford, consisting of cane, oil and paints: also a quantity of flagg in Hartford."

Lambert Hitchcock transferred to Rufus Holmes, Theron Rockwell, Jesse Ives, and William L. Holabird his property in trust. The trustees were to sell, manage, and dispose of the property in a manner most beneficial to his creditors, while he continued to carry on the chair business as agent, with success, for we read in the *Hartford Courant*, under date of November 27, 1832,

"Notice is hereby given that the chair business lately carried on by Lambert Hitchcock as agent is now resumed by him on his own account and responsibility, and that his trustees are no longer interested in or responsible for the same. The subscriber will continue to manufacture chairs, and now has on hand a large and elegant assortment of chairs, made after the latest fashions, and finished in the best manner.

LAMBERT HITCHCOCK

Hitchcocksville, November 17, 1832."

Under the date, July 20, 1828,

"Lambert Hitchcock and Samuel Couch of Barkhamsted, co-partners of the firm of Hitchcock and Couch, being justly indebted and being rendered by misfortunes unable to pay," made assignment to the same trustees as did Lambert Hitchcock, all of their co-partnership effects, "consisting principally of an assortment of dry goods, drugs and medicines lately purchased, and now in the brick building standing in Hitchcocksville nearly opposite the said Hitchcock factory, also a

6

quantity of lumber and brick purchased for the purpose of rebuilding our store which was recently burned, and one ox cart.

Signed

LAMBERT HITCHCOCK
SAMUEL COUCH."

In the report of the Commissioners on relations of Lambert Hitchcock to the Superior Court of articles "sold for the benefit of the creditors," is a long list of his books, with the prices brought. It is interesting to find that the list includes, Scott's *Napoleon*, three volumes; Johnson's *Lives of the Poets*, three volumes; Boswell's *Johnson; Washington's Letters;* Milton's *Poetical Works*, three volumes; *Life of Franklin;* Watt's *On the Mind;* Homer's *Iliad;* Reid *On the Mind.*

Arba Alford, Junior, who had been employed by Lambert Hitchcock from the time he went into business, soon becoming production manager, was taken into partnership, and the business was continued, making the same type of chairs, but the name on the back was changed to "Hitchcock, Alford & Co., Warranted." Mr. Alford attended to the shop, while Mr. Hitchcock spent most of his time selling the products of the factory, travelling much through the South, New England, and the Western states.

Meanwhile Lambert Hitchcock had married, October 30, 1830, one of Hitchcocksville's comely young women, Eunice Alford, a sister of his partner, and one of the five daughters of Arba Alford, who had come from Simsbury in 1795, and settled on the west bank of the Farmington River.

Lambert Hitchcock and his partner built a large house across from the chair factory. This house is of unusual interest, as a solid brick wall divides it, running from the cellar to the attic, with the rooms on either side identical. On the west side of the house a wing was built for the mother of Eunice Hitchcock and Arba Alford, who had been left a widow in 1823. No doors connect the Hitchcock and Alford homes; only in the wing built for the mother is there any door between the two parts.

In a diary with yellowed leaves, in the quaint phraseology of the time, penned by Eunice Hitchcock from the time of her marriage until her death, some light is thrown on her husband's frequent business trips, and much is written of the love and devotion of this man and woman of a hundred years ago. Under date of June 29, 1831, Eunice Hitchcock writes: "My dear Companion is now gone to Cheshire, his native place, after his mother and I am quite lonely and dejected. He started this morning about 2 o'clock. I feel quite uneasy about him on account of the horse he has gone with, which is quite unsteady." April 29, 1832, we read, "My dear husband has this day started for New York. Expects to be absent some time. I felt quite loath to have him go. We both shed tears." April 30, 1833, she writes, "My husband has again started for New York accompanied by Brother Arba to buy goods for the ensuing season." On June 6 Lambert Hitchcock had been "absent five weeks on business," and Eunice writes "which time I felt very lonely but enjoyed my mind most of the time. On September 5, 1834 moved to Hartford. Had a very comfortable time, though somewhat muddy."

This record of a woman's love and hopes and ambitions was kept up to the night before her death, April 1, 1835, when her last written word was "An acrostic to my Husband," and underneath, in Lambert Hitchcock's beautiful handwriting is, "Eunice died last night." She was taken back to Hitchcocksville, where she sleeps in the

quiet little cemetery near the home where most of her short life of thirty years was lived.

In 1834 Lambert Hitchcock was a representative to the General Assembly from Barkhamsted, and the same year Mr. and Mrs. Hitchcock took up their residence in Hartford, living on Trumbull Street. The diary shows that they left Hitchcocksville in order that Mr. Hitchcock might be near the "center of things" for his business trips, but going often to Hitchcocksville, as the diary shows. By 1832 over one hundred stagecoach lines ran out from Boston, and only a little later twenty-two lines had their headquarters in Hartford; while in 1835 several railroads were opened, and with the well-equipped boat service from Hartford, it was an ideal place for this manufacturer to make his home. Many items in Eunice Hitchcock's diary concerning these trips are of great interest, and show the territory through which he travelled in selling his chairs, and explain why so many "Hitchcocks" are found throughout the country.

Lambert Hitchcock wrote to his partner, under date of October 29, 1835, from Chicago, Illinois.

(Postmarked Chicago, November 3.)
"To Mr. Arba Alford, Hitchcocksville, Connecticut.
Dear friend:

Thursday morning last I arrived in Chicago from Detroit, after a journey of thirteen days, not on the most direct route to this place, but winding through the territory from one point to another at which I wished to stop. My first visit on my arrival was to go to the office for letters. The evening mail which arrives every other day from Detroit brought your letter, and I can assure you I was very glad to receive it. If this letter is as long coming to you, I might about as well bring it myself, for within that time I expect to be pretty well on my way home. The day after I wrote you from Detroit I saddled my pony and without company took my departure for Chicago." [A description follows, giving the general idea of the country and the different kinds of land in the territory of Michigan, "(about to become a state.)" giving a description of the settlers of that territory, many living in tents, and some living in "covered wagons" until shelter could be built. He writes], "Having rode my pony into the western part of Michigan, his back became so sore I was obliged to sell him. Here I fell in company with two young men merchants from the state of New York, who were also coming on to Chicago. Some part of the distance we came on foot, some of the way by stage, and occasionally we would hire a man to bring us on a few miles." [He writes of meeting Indians on the way, of continuing with his] "companions 'til we arrived in Chicago, the London of the west, as some of the inhabitants call it: a place of considerable business and contains between four and five thousand inhabitants. There are from twenty to twenty-five lawyers, but these study speculation more than speeches. There are twelve physicians, six clergymen and mechanics; a general assortment, among which are three chairmakers. It is not that I feel indifferent to our business at home that I say so little about it in this letter, but I wrote you at considerable length about it from Detroit, and have not much to add at this time. I trust it will receive in all its branches your constant and strict attention." [I am] "to pursue my way down the Illinois River to St. Louis: after staying a few days at that place, expect to return home by way of Cincinnati, Pittsburg and Philadelphia without much delay on the route. My respects to all friends,

Yours truly,
LAMBERT HITCHCOCK"

While on a trip South to sell chairs, Lambert Hitchcock stopped off for a few days in Washington, and under date of December 6, 1841, wrote again to Mr. Arba Alford.

"Dear Sir:

I arrived in Washington from Baltimore last evening and put up at Brown's Hotel. The houses of Congress came together to-day at 12 o'clock, and I have just returned from the

Capital, after spending two or three hours, most of the time in the Senate Chamber." [He speaks of seeing Henry Clay of Kentucky, James Buchanan of Pennsylvania and John Calhoun.]

"About this time one of the doorkeepers came to me and asked if I was a privileged character. I told him I had been informed a state senator would be permitted to remain on the floor of the Senate Chamber. He said 'certainly,' and after taking my name left me in the quiet possession of a seat much more comfortable than a crowded gallery. This gave me a very good opportunity to see and hear what was going on. The meeting of senators seemed very cordial, and there seemed much less of personal feeling among political opponents than might be supposed from the angry tones of their debating." [Monday evening he went to the President's house, with Mr. Smith.] "From the outer door we were conducted into the large hall by a servant. Here we were met by the son of the President, who conducted us into the Drawing Room, and introduced us to the President and Mrs. Tyler, the son's wife, who does the honors of the house, the President's wife being in ill health at this time. I expect to leave for Winchester (S.C.) Wednesday morning. I am in hopes it will not be necessary for me to remain there more than a week, but shall stay as long as a thorough attention to business may seem to require.

Yours truly,

LAMBERT HITCHCOCK"

In 1840 and 1841 Lambert Hitchcock was a state senator from the fifteenth district, which included at that time the towns of Litchfield, Harwinton, New Hartford, Torrington, Winchester, Barkhamsted, and Colebrook.

The firm name of Hitchcock, Alford & Company was kept until the early forties, when Lambert Hitchcock left the firm and went to Unionville, where he continued to manufacture chairs of the same construction and decoration as the Hitchcocksville ones, but these were marked "Lambert Hitchcock, Unionville, Connecticut."

Lambert Hitchcock remarried in 1836, at Cazenovia, New York, Mary Ann Preston, and had three sons and a daughter. One of the sons, Major Henry Preston Hitchcock, born at Hitchcocksville, was a well-known business man of Hartford.

Lambert Hitchcock died in 1852, ~~having manufactured chairs for forty-three years~~, and in his will requested that Arba Alford, his former partner, should be executor of his estate.

After Mr. Hitchcock left the firm, Arba Alford took into partnership his brother Alfred, where the same type of chairs made by the old firm were put out under the name of Alford & Company. Here, too, in a wing of the factory, Alford & Company conducted a general store.

The chair factory at Hitchcocksville was sold about 1864 to Leroy and Delos Stephens, who manufactured pocket rulers for nearly forty years.

The quiet little town of Hitchcocksville, lying snugly between the hills, where lazily flows the Farmington, was Hitchcocksville until 1866, when because of the similarity of the name of Hotchkissville, the name was changed to Riverton. The Hitchcocksville factory is standing as in the old days, but now houses a rubber factory, while across from it is the lovely old Hitchcock-Alford homestead, with its open fireplaces and brick ovens, a charming home where lives the family of an Alford descendant.

Lightning Source UK Ltd.
Milton Keynes UK
UKHW010633141120
373360UK00002B/794